HONG K
THE CITY AT A

MN00324767

INTRODUCTION
THE CHANGING FACE OF THE URBAN SCENE

Almost two decades since Hong Kong was returned by its British rulers to a resurgent China, the struggle to determine the quasi-independent city's identity has only intensified. At times it seems that nearly everything is fodder for emotionally heated debate: the extent of political freedoms; how many tourists is too many; whether the traditionally hands-off government should do more, or less, to rein in property prices and pollution.

Amid all these tensions it's easy to lose track of the fact that, as ever, Hong Kong has a lot going for it – and there are even signs of improvement. Its uneasy position on China's geographical and political fringes, its concentration of affluence and a sophisticated consumer set make it a powerful magnet for restaurateurs, artists, designers and others seeking to blaze a path in an ascending Asia; entire neighbourhoods are evolving under their influence. Beyond the backstreets, progress on big-ticket projects such as the M+ museum (see p064), and the transformation of the colonial-era Police Married Quarters (see p037) into a design incubation hub, point to a new determination to become the region's creative core. And, of course, Hong Kong's time-honoured charms – its dramatic skyline, deep-water bays, striking peaks and pulsating streets – are still firmly in place. As the deadline for integration with mainland China draws closer, the sense that the city may be operating on borrowed time has heightened its air of restless dynamism.

ESSENTIAL INFO
FACTS, FIGURES AND USEFUL ADDRESSES

TOURIST OFFICE
The Peak Piazza
T 2508 1234
www.discoverhongkong.com

TRANSPORT
Airport transfer to city centre
Airport Express trains depart every 10
minutes between 5.50am and 12.45am.
The journey takes about 25 minutes
Car hire
Avis
T 2882 2927
Metro
Trains run from roughly 6am to 1am daily
www.mtr.com.hk
Taxis
Cab ranks are located throughout the city
or you can hail a taxi on the street
Travel card
A three-day pass costs HK$300 and
includes unlimited MTR travel and two
single journeys on the Airport Express

EMERGENCY SERVICES
Ambulance/Fire/Police
T 999
Late-night pharmacy
Mannings
Shop B
517 Jaffe Road
T 2574 5483

CONSULATES
British Consulate-General
1 Supreme Court Road
T 2901 3000
www.gov.uk/government/world/hong-kong
US Consulate-General
26 Garden Road
T 2523 9011
hongkong.usconsulate.gov

POSTAL SERVICES
Post office
2 Connaught Place
T 2921 2222
Shipping
UPS
T 2735 3535
www.ups.com

BOOKS
An Insular Possession by Timothy Mo
(Paddleless Press)
Architecture of Density by Michael Wolf
(Peperoni Books)
Gweilo by Martin Booth (Bantam)

WEBSITES
Arts
www.hkac.org.hk
Newspaper
www.scmp.com

EVENTS
Art Basel Hong Kong
www.artbasel.com
Business of Design Week
www.bodw.com
Detour
www.detour.hk

COST OF LIVING
**Taxi from Hong Kong International
Airport to city centre**
HK$350
Cappuccino
HK$35
Packet of cigarettes
HK$54
Daily newspaper
HK$8
Bottle of champagne
HK$1,000

HONG KONG
Population
7.2 million
Currency
Hong Kong dollar
Telephone code
Hong Kong: 852
Local time
GMT +8
Flight time
London: 12 hours

CHINA

Tokyo
Beijing · Seoul
Shanghai
Delhi
Taipei
Hanoi □ Hong Kong
Mumbai
Bangkok

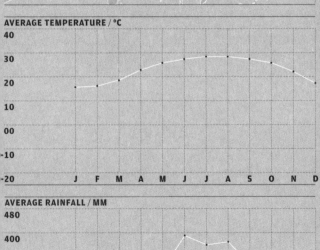

AVERAGE TEMPERATURE / °C

40												
30												
20												
10												
00												
-10												
-20	J	F	M	A	M	J	J	A	S	O	N	D

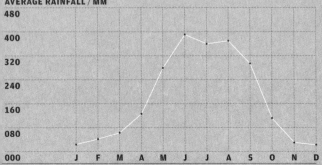

AVERAGE RAINFALL / MM

480												
400												
320												
240												
160												
080												
000	J	F	M	A	M	J	J	A	S	O	N	D

NEIGHBOURHOODS

THE AREAS YOU NEED TO KNOW AND WHY

To help you navigate the city, we've chosen the most interesting districts (see below and the map inside the back cover) and colour-coded our featured venues, according to their location; those venues that are outside these areas are not coloured.

WEST KOWLOON

On the western side of Kowloon, there's a waterfront promenade perfect for biking or jogging. Make the W (see p016) and its supercool Woobar lounge (T 3717 2889), your base, and witness one of Asia's most ambitious construction programmes: the emergence of the West Kowloon Cultural District, already heralded by the ICC (see p013), will complete the transformation of this grade-A harbourside land.

TSIM SHA TSUI

The southern tip of Kowloon is the setting for David Yeo's preservation success story, 1881 Heritage, where you'll find Hullett House (see p016) and many restaurants, bars and shops. Also here is the venerable Peninsula hotel (see p020) and the area's main drag, Nathan Road. Start exploring TST's nascent art scene at K11 Art Mall (18 Hanoi Road, T 3118 8070), a mix of galleries and stores showing work by Asian artists.

CAUSEWAY BAY/HAPPY VALLEY

Here are two very different zones, pulling in two very different directions. Causeway Bay has long been characteristic of the hyperactive Hong Kong experience; buzzy boutiques at street level, and eateries and lounges hidden away on upper floors that offer respite from the madness. Happy Valley has changed into a kind of super-suburb, defined as much by its exclusive apartments and neighbourhood cafés as its world-famous racecourse (see p090).

MID-LEVELS

Soho isn't half as fashionable as it might have been, nor as it would like to be, but its themed shopping streets are still fun to explore, each distinctive in its personality. Don't stop there, though. Only in Hong Kong would you find a super-efficient escalator system whisking commuters 800m down Victoria Peak into Central during the morning rush hour, and back up the slopes again after work.

CENTRAL

This district is the epitome of what we in the West expect from Hong Kong: the skyscrapers, the sophistication, the shoppers. Many visitors never venture anywhere else, and you can see why. Stay at The Putman (see p022) or The Upper House (see p024), go boutique-hopping in Noho and sample the area's culinary delights, from the *dai pai dong* (street-food stalls) to Lung King Heen (see p053).

ABERDEEN/STANLEY PENINSULA

It's always surprising how close the real countryside is to the heart of the city. The south of Hong Kong Island has its secluded nooks and crannies, sand and barefoot boîtes, although getting there at the weekend can be a chore. Spend a lazy afternoon on Shek O Beach (see p089) or lose a few hours at the Sense of Touch spa (109 Repulse Bay Road, T 2592 9668). Beware of the celebrated Stanley Market; it has its supporters but it's a tourist trap.

LANDMARKS

THE SHAPE OF THE CITY SKYLINE

Hong Kong is not a difficult city in which to orient yourself. The best way is to take the Peak Tram (www.thepeak.com.hk) from Central up to Victoria Peak mountain; go during the day to see as far as the islands of Macau (see p100) or late at night to dodge the crowds. The Peak itself lacks any standout attractions, but there is no disputing the scenic view – a rush of high-rise style. Hundreds of towers are set against the backdrop of the ocean, in such lush surrounds that it seems they shouldn't be there at all. From here, you can look across the harbour, which has diminished in size over the past few years as land has been reclaimed to host the new Central waterfront and the West Kowloon Cultural District. The harbourside promenade stretches from the Central piers to the Tamar site in Admiralty, where the government's new HQ was completed in 2011. The Peak still serves as a pretty accurate social altimeter – the higher up you live, the more money, Range Rovers and pictures in *Hong Kong Tatler* you've accrued.

The other essential navigation device is the justly famous ferry. Linking Hong Kong Island and Kowloon since the 1880s, the Star Ferry (www.starferry.com.hk) is a functional necessity, both in terms of transport and mental respite. Its importance should not be underestimated. Locals still remember when the ludicrously low fares were raised by just five cents in 1966 and riots broke out. *For full addresses, see Resources.*

HighCliff

Just pipped by Norman Foster's Gherkin in London for the year's prestigious Emporis Skyscraper Award when it was completed in 2003, this 73-storey apartment block (one of the tallest residential buildings in Hong Kong) is 252m high and serves as an excellent reference point in the leafy and desirable suburb of Happy Valley. Its thin, rather rakish profile was successful in earning architects Dennis Lau and Ng Chun Man a host of other international prizes. Unfortunately, HighCliff's 113 apartments are better appreciated from the outside than inside, where the design has largely been toned down in order to appeal to the conservative tastes of the local financial community — the only people who are wealthy enough to afford the eye-wateringly steep rents.

41d Stubbs Road, www.highcliff.com.hk

Apartment blocks

They might not be the most immediately attractive aspect of the Hong Kong skyline, but they are arguably its most distinctive feature. When you step off the plane at the gleaming International Airport, the impossibly impersonal geometries of rows upon rows of prefab apartment blocks are one of the first things you will see. On the drive into town, they heave rapidly into view, and their towering bulk informs any walk around Wan Chai or even the bustling shopping district of Mong Kok. In the badlands of the New Territories, they're practically the default vernacular. These high-rises (Central Park Towers, above left) sprang up in the 1950s and 1960s as a hurried response to the huge pressures on housing in the colony and here they remain, a visual marker of today's emphatically urban society.

ICC

The West Kowloon waterfront is like a gap waiting for the final piece in a very high-stakes jigsaw puzzle. When the land here is finally filled by Foster + Partners' delay-ridden West Kowloon Cultural District, due to open in phases from roughly 2020 at a cost of HK$23bn, the takeover of Hong Kong's prime harbour-facing land will be complete. The kingpin is the International Commerce Centre (ICC), the city's tallest building at 484m. Kohn Pedersen Fox and Wong & Ouyang's striking edifice, housing office, residential and retail space, sits above Kowloon MTR Station, which links to the exclusive Elements shopping mall via a vast atrium. Its 100th-floor observation deck competes with the Peak for the city's best view, and The Ritz-Carlton (see p016) holds sway over the top 16 floors.
1 Austin Road West, www.shkp-icc.com

Two IFC

Two International Finance Centre (IFC) opened in 2004 at the height of Hong Kong's post-SARS depression, and the developers almost had to give the office space away. In something of a panic, a deal was cobbled together to entice UBS, an investment bank, to take 15,800 sq m at a rumoured price of HK$140 to HK$200 per sq m per month. By 2006, an unnamed tenant was renewing its lease in this very same building for HK$1,300 per sq m, and vacancy for the 93,000 sq m office space remains limited, despite the corporate shift out of Central in recent years. Built on reclaimed land, the 412m-high tower is part of a complex that encompasses One IFC, also designed by Cesar Pelli and completed in 1998, the Four Seasons (see p030) and the IFC Mall (T 2295 3308).
8 Finance Street, www.ifc.com.hk

One Peking

Some say it resembles a cut-price Burj Al Arab – all steel and glass with a facade like a billowing sail. In truth, Rocco Design Architects' 30-storey tower is not the most sophisticated piece of architecture ever built, but when it was completed in 2003 it was a symbol of the new Kowloon – a once low-rise zone now filling up with daring skyscrapers. One Peking tops out at 160m, and a large proportion of it is solar-powered. It was environmentally friendly credentials such as these that caught the attention of Hong Kong's Institute of Architects and, in 2003, the building was the recipient of its Medal of the Year. Numerous luxury boutiques, bars and restaurants are to be found inside, including Aqua Spirit (T 3427 2288) and Hutong (T 3428 8342).

1 Peking Road, www.onepeking.com.hk

HOTELS

WHERE TO STAY AND WHICH ROOMS TO BOOK

The cross-tunnel traffic can be a little frenetic, so your first decision should be on which side of the harbour to base yourself. Central is sleeker, but the view from Kowloon at night is one of the world's great sights. And nowhere more so than from The Ritz-Carlton (ICC, 1 Austin Road West, T 2263 2263); its 103rd-floor lobby is reached by a 52-second lift journey. Nearby, the W (1 Austin Road West, T 3717 2222) also strengthens Kowloon's case. Meanwhile, the fleet of green Rolls-Royces at The Peninsula (see p020) shines bright, and Hullett House (1881 Heritage, 2a Canton Road, T 3988 0000) has a similar aura of breezy colonial sophistication. Further afield, Pentahotel (19 Luk Hop Street, T 3112 8222) brings a touch of minimalist style to emerging Kai Tak, the site of the former airport.

On Hong Kong Island, the eco-conscious design and generous rooms of The Upper House (see p024) are doing their best to shift the emphasis away from business-driven efficiency towards an enveloping sense of calm. Luxury boutique properties are on the rise – following the lead of J Plus (1-5 Irving Street, T 3196 9000), formerly JIA, and the late Andrée Putman's The Putman (see p022), are The Jervois (opposite) and Hotel Indigo (246 Queen's Road East, T 3926 3888), a slick addition to a district that is gentrifying at a rapid rate. For a low-budget alternative, ascetic creative types swear by the trusty YMCA (41 Salisbury Road, T 2268 7000).

For full addresses and room rates, see Resources.

The Jervois

Located in an otherwise unassuming corner of the tradition-rich Sheung Wan neighbourhood, the 36-storey Jervois stands out for several reasons, among them its ability to impart a welcome sense of space in a city where it is sorely lacking. Designer Christian Liaigre equipped the 49 suites (Two-Bedroom Suite, above) with expansive windows and minimalist fittings that strive to be unobtrusive, yet convey luxury via elements of leather and dark wood. Billed as serviced apartments, The Jervois is well-equipped for short-term stays; kitchenettes and an abundance of esteemed restaurants in the vicinity, such as the famed claypot rice specialist Hap Shing (T 2850 5723), help to compensate for the lack of on-site dining options. *89 Jervois Street, T 3994 9000, www.thejervois.com*

Mira Moon
This 2013 property takes its name from a goddess of Chinese legend. Wanders & yoo took that as a cue to reference local traditions in rooms like the New Moon King (pictured), mixing peony motifs and dark wood furnishings with glossy surfaces and ceramic curios. Add views of Victoria Harbour and you've an ideal base in the increasingly chic Wan Chai.
388 Jaffe Road, T 2643 8888

The Peninsula

The undisputed grande dame of Hong Kong's hotel scene, the 1928 Peninsula embarked on an ambitious renovation in 2012 that aimed to keep the old girl looking fresh. While historical tradition has been retained in the neoclassical flourishes of the vast lobby (opposite), the guest rooms (Grand Deluxe Kowloon View Room, above) have seen a greater transformation, as stiff formality has given way to contemporary interiors. The infrastructure is equally modern – rooms are serviced via tablets that can control everything from mood lighting to room-service menus. Another highlight is the Felix (T 2696 6778), an innovative French restaurant designed by Philippe Starck, which grows ever more freewheeling as the evening develops. *Salisbury Road, T 2920 2888, www.peninsula.com*

The Putman

Upscale hotels dominate the Hong Kong accommodation scene, but medium-term visitors would do well to consider some of the city's serviced-apartment options. Among the finest is The Putman, named after its designer, Andrée, and located on the edge of Central and the up-and-coming Sheung Wan. Putman stamped her trademark minimalism on the 28 units, using clean, neutral colours and white for the interiors, which are flooded with light through the floor-to-ceiling windows. The One-Bedroom Suites (above) each contain one of her 'Crescent Moon' sofas and, in the airy bathrooms, Villeroy & Boch standalone bathtubs and Dornbracht rain showers complete the feeling of perfectly pitched luxury.
202 Queen's Road Central, T 2233 2233, www.theputman.com

The Upper House

Hong Kong is a city that can, in part, be defined by the frequently overused close-door buttons in its lifts, such is the sense of urgency. It's significant, then, that The Upper House has left them out. Hong Kong-born designer André Fu has excelled here, creating a 117-room urban retreat that has a feel of calm and quiet luxury, employing natural colours and tastefully selected materials (shoji glass, lacquered paper panels and limed oak flooring). The hotel occupies the top 12 floors of a 49-storey building, and a sky bridge connects Café Gray Deluxe (T 3968 1106) and the Sky Lounge, both of which afford stunning views. If you can't secure one of the two penthouses (above), settle for the 114 sq m Upper Suite.

Pacific Place, 88 Queensway, T 2918 1838, www.upperhouse.com

Hotel Icon

The 2011 opening of this boutique-meets-business hotel in Kowloon was yet another indication that Hong Kong's centre of gravity is gradually shifting away from the bright lights of Central. The lobby (above), decked out in glistening white marble and dominated by a dramatic spiral staircase, makes it clear that Hotel Icon can compete with any of its rivals. Plump for the Club 36 Harbour room (overleaf) and you'll be treated to interiors influenced by the Chinese philosophy of yin and yang, and panoramic views of Victoria Harbour. The intriguing dining options – including Green (T 3400 1300), a café/bar next to an indoor vertical garden – as well as the top-notch Angsana Spa (see p093) may mean you'll never feel the need to cross the water.
17 Science Museum Road, T 3400 1000,
www.hotel-icon.com

Club 36 Harbour, Hotel Icon

Landmark Mandarin Oriental

Home to some of the city's largest rooms, not to mention being next door to Harvey Nichols (T 3695 3388), the Landmark also offers a 2,320 sq m spa (T 2132 0011) and the acclaimed two-Michelin-starred French restaurant Amber (T 2132 0066), which is a firm favourite with big-spending locals. The low-level lighting and earth tones in the lobby (above) and throughout the hotel will almost make you forget its one glaring deficiency: there are no views to speak of. However, there's little question that the standard of comfort and finish in the rooms, such as the L450 Deluxe (opposite), is as good as you will find in Hong Kong; and the concierge service is slightly younger and savvier than at some of the Island's more traditional hotels. *15 Queen's Road, T 2132 0188, www.mandarinoriental.com/landmark*

Four Seasons
Many visitors have stayed at HK's Four Seasons and never even set foot outside. Linked to the IFC complex (see p014), it possesses spacious rooms – such as the Deluxe Harbour-View (pictured) – and an impressive Executive Club Lounge on the 45th floor. The Airport Express train station is only a 10-minute walk away. *8 Finance Street, T 3196 8888, www.fourseasons.com/hongkong*

24 HOURS

SEE THE BEST OF THE CITY IN JUST ONE DAY

Nearly every day in Hong Kong will involve a journey across the harbour – a brief but monumental trip proving that the best things in life are (almost) free. We begin in the Mid-Levels, with a spot of retail and cultural therapy, followed by lunch at 22 Ships (see p036) or Watermark (Central Pier 7, T 2167 7251), which has views across the bay. Unlike Beijing, Hong Kong is no artistic trendsetter, but there are gems to be found in industrial Kwun Tong, including Osage Gallery (Fourth floor, 20 Hing Yip Street, T 2793 4817), and Chai Wan, where Platform China (Sixth floor, Chai Wan Industrial City Phase 1, 60 Wing Tai Road, T 9768 8093) provides a bridge to the fertile scene across the border. On Hong Kong Island, an influx of Western galleries looking to connect to China has imbued the art scene with new vigour. Lehmann Maupin (407 Pedder Building, 12 Pedder Street, T 2530 0025) is a recent arrival, and has a modern Asian focus, while, in the same building, the Gagosian (Seventh floor, T 2151 0555) regularly features international luminaries.

It's also worth spending a few hours away from the metropolis. The biggest surprise to first-time visitors is not the perpetually photographed skyscape of Central, it's the enormous amount of unspoilt greenery within easy travelling distance of this Eastern Manhattan. The car-free island of Cheung Chau, for instance, is a short hop on the First Ferry (T 2131 8181, www.nwff.com.hk). *For full addresses, see Resources.*

11.00 Konzepp

Even for newcomers to the city, Konzepp won't prove hard to find: just look for the distinctive yellow facade that juts into an otherwise drab streetscape. The bar in the rough-edged semi-basement space serves up impeccably brewed teas with chocolates and cookies, but that's not the only stimulation on offer. Launched in 2011 by local designer Geoff Tsui and film producer Willie Chan, the versatile outlet stocks clothing, bags and accessories from global taste vanguards such as Études and Seventy Eight Percent, hosts pop-up art events and is even known to throw the odd party. Some would accuse Konzepp of having an identity crisis, but we prefer to see it as a perennial work in progress, in the best possible sense.
50 Tung Street, T 2803 0339,
www.konzepp.com

12.00 Liang Yi Museum

In this cramped city, Liang Yi is a refuge, free of the throngs that crowd so many cultural sites. This is due to policies that are more rigorous than normal: visitors must call in advance to book a mandatory guided tour covered by the HK$200 entry fee, but the effort is worth it. The museum celebrates its place on the Hollywood Road antiques strip with a superb hoard of period Chinese furniture, mainly Ming and Qing Dynasty pieces from local tycoon Peter Fung's collection. The white-walled interiors ensure that focus is firmly on the craftwork, from the Imperial zitan screens (above) to the seats carved out of lustrous rosewood. Items are arranged as they would have been in ancient homes, and many look untouched by the centuries.
181-199 Hollywood Road, T 2806 8280, www.liangyimuseum.com

13.00 22 Ships

Opened in 2012 by Michelin-starred British chef Jason Atherton alongside Singaporean entrepreneur Yenn Wong, this unassuming tapas bar is one of a handful of restaurants now leading the gentrification of the once rather bawdy and down-at-heel Wan Chai. The venue has made the most of a slightly claustrophobic space, keeping the decor to a minimum and clustering several tiny (but functional) tables around an active central bar. Executive chef Nathan Green's modern take on Spanish cuisine includes the likes of baby squid with chorizo, red pepper and paprika, plus local staples such as pork belly. Ships' burgeoning reputation and no-booking policy mean it's constantly packed: great for energy levels, but make sure you arrive in good time or be prepared for lengthy queues. *22 Ship Street, T 2555 0722, www.22ships.hk*

15.00 PMQ

The Hong Kong government's record on preservation is mixed, but PMQ, the city's new home for 'create-preneurs', may set a template for a more balanced approach. A three-year effort to restore the colonial-era Police Married Quarters has resulted in an unprecedented amount of studio and retail space for artists and designers, the less established of whom qualify for subsidised rents. It's a great idea in a city where punishing overheads often stifle creativity. The warren-like corridors hold dozens of furniture-makers, jewellers and designers, like 794729 Metalwork (T 2803 0233) and YiLine (T 2526 8326), as well as bigger names such as Herman Miller. The night markets and pop-up exhibitions should keep things from getting staid.
35 Aberdeen Street, T 2811 9098,
www.pmq.org.hk

20.00 Ammo

Think tanks aren't known for generating a buzz, but the New York-based Asia Society turned that idea on its head with the 2012 opening of its Hong Kong outpost, set in a revitalised cluster of former British military buildings in Admiralty. Arguably the centre's crown jewel, bar/restaurant Ammo plays on the complex's past as an explosives warehouse, due to an interior that's heavy on ashen shades and metallic finishes, such as the massive copper ribs that seem to prop up the ceiling. The menu, overseen by local prodigy Tony Cheng, is a traditional take on European cuisine (handmade pastas, tapas) in a city better known for its questionable fusions. Things get more adventurous on the cocktail list, which includes only-in-HK creations – try the Likechee, a blend of vodka, lychee liqueur, lemon juice and jasmine syrup.
9 Justice Drive, T 2537 9888,
www.ammo.com.hk

URBAN LIFE

CAFÉS, RESTAURANTS, BARS AND NIGHTCLUBS

The irony of a megacity as in-your-face as Hong Kong is that even some of the finest dining and drinking venues have to advertise themselves because they're so hidden. The China Club restaurant (T 2521 8888), for example, is found on the 13th floor of the Old Bank of China Building (1 Bank Street). Similarly, Jason Atherton's Aberdeen Street Social (Ground floor, JPC, 35 Aberdeen Street, T 2866 0300) is tucked away in the gardens of PMQ (see p037). Hong Kong also loves its 'private kitchens', which, by their nature, can be tricky to locate; try Yin Yang (18 Ship Street, T 2866 0868) for authentic, organic Cantonese cuisine in a heritage setting.

Eat at least once in a classic diner such as Nam Kee Spring Roll Noodle Co (66-72 Stanley Street, T 2576 8007), as well as excellent new-wave restaurant The Chairman (18 Kau U Fong, T 2555 2202). The Western District's high-style venues include street-art-centric French establishment Bibo (163 Hollywood Road, T 2956 3188), while Chachawan (206 Hollywood Road, T 2549 0020) serves searingly authentic Thai food in a vintage shophouse atmosphere.

Wyndham Street is the upscale counterpart to Central's party strip, Lan Kwai Fong, and its monied ambience is tangible. Mingle with models at burlesque-themed club Bisous (Ninth floor, LKF Tower, No 33, T 2501 0002), or sup spirits and cocktails at lounge bar The Blck Brd (Sixth floor, 8 Lyndhurst Terrace, T 2545 8555). *For full addresses, see Resources.*

Duddell's

No single venue can claim to have it all, but that hasn't stopped Duddell's from trying. The property's list of ambitions include thriving art space, buzzing bar and supplier of fine Cantonese cuisine, in a city with no shortage of contenders to all three crowns. On a recent visit we took in a mixed-media art exhibition; surveyed the financial district from a verdant terrace, gin-based cocktail in hand; and indulged in what might be the definitive versions of local delicacies like braised pork belly and fried lobster. All this in Ilse Crawford's lovely multistorey space, which combines natural wood, travertine and vintage flourishes. Small wonder that Duddell's has become a nexus of the city's creative network.
Level 3, 1 Duddell Street, T 2525 9191, www.duddells.co

The Pawn
This colonial-minded pub resides in a restored early 20th-century tenement block, and is the place to go if you're in the mood for modern British fare and a nice selection of lagers. Artist Stanley Wong's interiors pay careful attention to the original features, lending the venue a vital air of authenticity; there is also a glorious garden on the roof.
62 Johnston Road, T 2866 3444

Nocturne

This Japanese-inspired speakeasy is hardly a secret – the name is carved on the door for all to see, and no passwords or prior reservations are required. But it still has a clandestine feel. Candlelight illuminates the minimalist concrete surfaces and the hushed jazz notes encourage patrons to kick back and unwind. An impressive range of wines and whiskies, including Japanese and Scottish single-malts, and small-batch US bourbons, is available at reasonable prices. The fare also includes a limited but classy range of nibbles such as cheese, sashimi and Ibérico ham. Very rarely overcrowded and always welcoming, Nocturne is an exercise in understatement in a neighbourhood that more typically caters to brash big-spenders.

35 Peel Street, T 2884 9566,
www.nocturnehk.com

Yardbird

It's rare that the humble chicken is given gushing praise, but then few eateries approach it with as much inventiveness or dissect it with such superior skill as this red-hot Sheung Wan restaurant. Cheerful but no-frills decor – large windows, bar stools, and menus tacked on to the white walls – contribute to its casual vibe. The real artistry is in the food, which consists almost exclusively of *yakitori* (skewered chicken pieces). From creamy liver to a salt-and-pepper-dusted tail, nothing is wasted, and the results are delicious. Yardbird's other selling points include a no-reservation, no-service-charge policy, as well as one of the city's better collections of sake, craft beer and whisky. Come early, and be prepared to linger. *33-35 Bridges Street, T 2547 9273, www.yardbirdrestaurant.com*

Cafe Post
The star restaurant at Hotel Indigo (see p016) has generated as many plaudits as the stylish property itself, for both its cheery atmosphere and artful balance of Chinese and Western cuisine. Throw in some of the best coffee on the island, courtesy of accomplished local roasters Rabbithole, and it's no wonder so many tired professionals flock here every day.
246 Queen's Road East, T 3926 3988

Quinary

When it opened in 2012, Quinary promised a 'scientific' approach to cocktail making, but thankfully this buzzing spot has proved to be far from antiseptic. Mellow lighting, opulent leather sofas, metal latticework and steamer trunks impart a comfortable, lived-in air. The long bar is fitted with a range of top-end spirits and sophisticated gear – a caviar box, a rotary evaporator and centrifuges are just a selection of the equipment used to make the concoctions here. And what concoctions they are: head bartender Antonio Lai's innovative flavour combinations lead to such idiosyncratic libations as a wasabi-tinged Bloody Mary and an Earl Grey Caviar Martini, both of which encapsulate Quinary's fine balance of sophistication and decadence.
56-58 Hollywood Road, T 2851 3223,
www.quinary.hk

Ozone

In a city where soaring skyscrapers are de rigueur, The Ritz-Carlton atop West Kowloon's ICC (see p013) is the jewel in the crown, staking its claim to be the loftiest hotel in the world, with the highest bar in the world (at the time of writing, anyway). Its 118th-floor Ozone bar is a destination in itself, not least for the outdoor terrace and the stunning 360-degree views across Hong Kong Island, Victoria Harbour and the South China Sea. The high-energy interior, with its edgy white honeycomb-patterned partitioning and ceiling, was designed by Japanese firm Wonderwall. If the excitement gets too much, head down 15 floors to the chocolate-centric Café 103 to indulge in delicious sweet and savoury cocoa-infused treats, along with drinks and afternoon tea.
*118th floor, ICC, 1 Austin Road West,
T 2263 2270, www.ritzcarlton.com*

Serge et le Phoque

From its location on the fringes of a wet market to a lack of signage and the breezy decor (natural wood and spearmint-green booths), it's clear Serge et le Phoque isn't trying hard to impress. But given that it's overseen by chef Christophe Pelé, who cut his teeth at Paris' Michelin-starred La Bigarrade, and has a relentless focus on quality, it inevitably became the culinary talk of the town. Elements of the menu are decidedly French – artisanal cheeses, beef from Parisian butchers – but there are concessions to the wider environment. Many dishes incorporate seafood flown in from Japan and are garnished with the likes of yuzu and sesame. The *prix-fixe* menu changes monthly, so you can never be certain what awaits, but rest assured it will be inventive and memorable.

Shop B2, 3 Wanchai Road, T 5465 2000

Lung King Heen

This was the first Chinese restaurant in the world to be awarded Michelin's ultimate three-star honour, bestowed in its inaugural Hong Kong guide in 2009. Head chef, Chan Yan Tak, doesn't have any formal culinary training but there can be no doubting his skills as he delivers super-fresh contemporary Cantonese cuisine: dim sum and seafood are his specialities. Chhada Siembieda & Associates' interior is delightful in its understated simplicity, given a lift by the glamorous silver-leaf ceiling. The restaurant is located in the Four Seasons hotel (see p030), so try to get a table by the wide glass windows for excellent harbour views, or take it up a notch in the private dining room that seats 14. Reserve well in advance.
Fourth floor, Four Seasons, 8 Finance Street, T 3196 8880, www.fourseasons.com

Sugar

Don't be fooled into thinking the only views worth considering in HK are from Central, Tsim Sha Tsui or The Peak. In 2010, Sugar opened its doors on the 32nd floor of the swish EAST hotel, proving that Hong Kong's skyline even looks spectacular away from the beaten tourist tracks. From the balcony on the east side of the bar, designed by William Lim of local firm CL3, the vista breaks out from the tyranny of the surrounding skyscrapers and stretches uninterrupted for miles towards Tai Tam. Possessing three tiers and an expansive terrace, Sugar is a choice spot to enjoy a sundowner or some fine wine and a few sharing plates. Snag one of the sofas and let the city enchant you. *32nd floor, EAST, 29 Taikoo Shing Road, T 3968 3738, www.sugar-hongkong.com*

Boqueria

Despite occupying one of Hong Kong's many vertical blocks, Boqueria does an admirable job of recreating the Barcelona happy-hour experience, bringing a much-needed dose of Mediterranean languor to the teeming streets of Central since it opened in 2012. Walls are decked out in a combination of dark wood and Moorish tiles; dried peppers and *jamón ibérico* hang down from the ceiling; and the day's specials are scrawled on blackboards. The food is equally unadulterated: wooden platters arrive bursting with plump olives, sharp cheeses and beautifully aged hams, to be washed down with what could be the city's longest list of Spanish wines. The trend for tapas is booming – 10 minutes away is Catalunya (T 2866 7900), a Spanish restaurant and bar opened in 2013 by elBulli alumnus Alain Devahive Tolosa. *Seventh floor, LKF Tower, 33 Wyndham Street, T 2321 8681, www.boqueria.com.hk*

Ronin

Having generated one of the city's biggest culinary buzzes in recent memory when they established Yardbird (see p045), the same team has made lightning strike twice with this take on the Japanese *izakaya*. Tucked away behind a blank slate door, Ronin plays refined sibling to its raucous sister venue, and is dominated by dim lighting and a long, stately wooden bar. That said, the vibe is anything but distant: reggae spills out of the stereo, and a range of fine sakes and *sochu* flows freely. The real highlight, however, is the food. While the small portions make it unwise to turn up too hungry, they also encourage the savouring of top-notch techniques. Dishes like flower crab with *uni* (sea urchin roe) deftly blend local and imported produce.
8 On Wo Lane, T 2547 5263,
www.roninhk.com

Mott 32

Mott 32 doesn't initially seem like a bastion of tradition. A spiral staircase opens on to a dark, cavernous juxtaposition of old-school China and Western gothic, in which antique chandeliers illuminate calligraphy-etched concrete and metallic cow skulls. Sit for a while, though, and familiar Hong Kong touches emerge. Despite the edgy veneer, this restaurant is respectful of the city's culinary heritage, its menu full of

Cantonese comfort dishes attaining new heights through painstakingly sourced ingredients. The *char siu* (barbecued pork) is butter-like in consistency, and a similar devotion to quality is apparent on the cocktail list, where such standards as an Old Fashioned are garnished with fresh flavours including shiso and goji berry.
4-4a Des Voeux Road, T 2885 8688, www.mott32.com

Dragon-i

Longevity is the rarest of commodities in Hong Kong's notoriously fickle club scene, which makes it all the more surprising that restaurant/lounge/club Dragon-i continues to pull the crowds after more than a decade in operation. Perhaps it was inevitable, since this is the one place that can claim to have a bit of everything: a tasty dim sum and Japanese menu that appeals to foodies; a critical mass of visiting big-name house and hip-hop acts to draw the scene-makers; and a glittery, contemporary-Asia-meets-1970s-disco design that still manages to look cool. The brainchild of designer India Mahdavi and clubbing impresario Gilbert Yeung, heir to HK entertainment tycoon Albert Yeung, Dragon-i looks set to remain a staple of the late-night circuit for years to come.
Upper ground floor, The Centrium,
60 Wyndham Street, T 3110 1222,
www.dragon-i.com.hk

INSIDER'S GUIDE

ANAIS-JOURDEN MAK CHUN TING, DESIGNER

Hong Kong-born and Paris-trained, Anais-Jourden Mak Chun Ting only founded her label, Jourden, in 2012, but she already has a following that includes local fashion icons like Hilary Tsui of Liger (see p074). Her bold, androgynous styles draw inspiration from the city's 'strange intersection of bourgeois and trashy'.

Mak takes lunch at the old-school Ser Wong Fun (30 Cochrane Street, T 2543 1032), known for its snake soup but also 'excelling in fuss-free Chinese dishes'. For dinner, she enjoys local cooking with a contemporary twist at Little Bao (66 Staunton Street, T 2194 0202), particularly the pork belly *bao* (Chinese-style buns). Her favourite nightspot, Ping Pong 129 Gintoneria (129 Second Street, T 9158 1584), is a former table tennis hall reborn as a Spanish gin bar. 'Its cool interiors feature high ceilings, long stairways and quality drinks, minus the sometimes-annoying Central crowds.'

Mak's devotion to fashion has helped her to uncover the city's best retail secrets, many clustered around Sheung Wan. Although it looks 'slightly rundown and humble', Hang Hing May Jewellery Fashion Co (282 Queen's Road Central, T 2581 2248) sells a good second-hand range of labels like Miu Miu and YSL. A crash-course in local trends can be had at 'playful, hip' boutique GumGumGum (8-10 Cleveland Street, T 3486 7070), where Mak recently picked up a skateboard stool by street-art collective Start From Zero. *For full addresses, see Resources.*

ARCHITOUR

A GUIDE TO HONG KONG'S ICONIC BUILDINGS

Hong Kong is a city that works hard to be noticed. But it's not the architectural hotbed that the coffee-table tomes would have you believe. Want to tour Gio Ponti's famous Shui-Hing department store? Tough. It's just an office block now. The story is a spatial version of entrepreneurialism: the way Hong Kong has, via equal parts chance and planning, made use of its hyper-dense setting. To get a real feel of the city's architecture, visit the ant-farm-like public escalators, ladder streets and malls-within-skyscrapers, and modern works such as Taoho Design's Wing Kwong Pentecostal Holiness Church (22 Heng Lam Street, T 2338 3825), or Opus Hong Kong (53 Stubbs Road), Frank Gehry's residential development on The Peak. Herzog & de Meuron's similarly bold M+ museum is set to become a new modernist landmark upon its 2017 opening.

Meanwhile, the Urban Renewal Authority continues to chip away at Hong Kong's heritage. There have, however, been some small victories against the wrecking ball, and a few very successful regeneration projects, including David Yeo's transformation of the Victorian Marine Police HQ into the 1881 Heritage complex (Canton Road), and the Asia Society's overhaul of former British military facilities (see p038). The conversion of the Police Married Quarters (see p037) can be added to that list. Unfortunately, in many areas, fast-track development continues unabated.

For full addresses, see Resources.

Landmark East

One of the more striking legacies in a drive to create office space outside the crowded confines of Hong Kong Island, Landmark East's twin commercial towers of 40 and 43 storeys are now the defining feature of the heavily industrial Kwun Tong district. Designed by the US-based Arquitectonica and completed in 2008, both buildings have parallelogram brise-soleil covering their north and south elevations, and each affords tenants sweeping views over Victoria Harbour. The complex's green credentials go well beyond its 3,251 sq m of gardens: its insulated, double-glazed windows are shaded with vertical fins to protect against the city's oppressive summer heat, and recycled rainwater is used to irrigate the landscaped areas.
100 How Ming Street,
www.landmarkeast.com.hk

Jockey Club Innovation Tower
The new home of Hong Kong Polytechnic University's design school is an emphatic statement of the city's intent to cement itself at the heart of Asia's burgeoning design industry. Conceived by Zaha Hadid and funded by the Jockey Club Charities Trust to the tune of HK$249m, the tower was completed in 2014 after nearly four years of construction. At 15 storeys, the structure is the tallest on the campus, its restless, fluid lines converging in a jutting crest that evokes a beacon, serving as a lightning-rod for creative talent across the region. The building also comprises some masterful practical touches, such as a large entry foyer with ample room for exhibitions, a near-porous exterior that layers glass-and-aluminum 'fins' to usher in plenty of natural light, and state-of-the-art studios and lecture halls.
11 Yuk Choi Road, T 2766 4925, www.sd.polyu.edu.hk

Jardine House

It's difficult to believe now, but for many years after it was completed in 1973, this 52-storey structure was the tallest building, not just in Hong Kong, but the whole of Asia. Indeed, everything about the office development spoke of excess. It was built on reclaimed land that was the most expensive in the world at the time and, because it was reclaimed, the foundations needed to be rethought.

The tower itself had to be super-light, and the design by Palmer & Turner (now known as P&T Group) was largely determined by these constraints – the porthole windows exist in order to reduce the weight. Metal cladding superseded the original glass mosaic tiles when they started falling off, and refurbishment in 1993 got rid of the 1970s interiors, more's the pity.
1 Connaught Place

Bank of China Tower

As Norman Foster's HSBC Building (Queen's Road Central) dwarfed the old Bank of China alongside it, so IM Pei's mirrored-glass, commu-capitalist replacement pipped its competitor in 1990. Foster's ode to suspension bridges, natural light and money cost US$1bn to complete, partly because of the need to reposition its foundations to accommodate the geomancers' diktats. Pei's rival edifice might have famously bad feng-shui, having been built on a steeply sloping plot, but its 72 storeys stand out amid Central's cluster of skyscrapers, and its gleaming glazed facade reflects the city back at itself. Given Hong Kong falls in a typhoon zone, Pei ensured the building could resist high-velocity winds due to an ingenious composite structural system.
1 Garden Road

Hong Kong Design Institute
This award-winning building, designed
by the French firm Coldefy & Associés
Architectes Urbanistes (CAAU), is one
of the best reasons to visit East Kowloon.
It features a massive 'sky city' platform
that appears to be floating on four inner
towers wrapped in white latticework.
These sit atop a grass-covered podium
that serves as a sort of urban park.
3 King Ling Road, T 3928 2000

SHOPPING

THE BEST RETAIL THERAPY AND WHAT TO BUY

Hong Kong is similar to Manhattan, not just in its island-bound density but in the way its inhabitants spend their money with gusto. Often there are queues just to get into the stores. So let's hear it for the fearsome shoppers of Hong Kong. Let's hear it, too, for the markets of Kowloon. The stalls are so thick on the ground and so crowded with stuff that there's hardly room to move.

Be sure to visit one of the city's many mega-malls, like Pacific Place (88 Queensway, T 2844 8900), a 650,000 sq m entertainment and retail complex upgraded in 2011 by British designer Thomas Heatherwick. If you're seeking out independent labels, Moustache (31 Aberdeen Street, T 2541 1955) utilises local sartorial expertise to create colonial-era-style cuts for men, whereas Soong Salon De Mode (Second floor, 8-10 Hankow Road, T 2723 1400) will copy vintage tailoring for women. Cool eyewear matters in this town, and Visual Culture (see p076) stocks a collection of crafted frames by coveted names. Nearby, Tina's Choice (Third floor, Lee Gardens One, 33 Hysan Avenue, T 2907 2688) provides an eclectic set of jewellery, handbags and other accessories. Rummagers may also want to indulge in the classic HK pastime of crate-digging for retro electronics and obscure camera gear at Sin Tat Plaza (83 Argyle Street). And don't miss the Noho area; the one-time home of Sun Yat-sen is fast filling up with one-off design and lifestyle stores. *For full addresses, see Resources.*

Jia Inc

Since its 2007 launch in Hong Kong by Taiwanese entrepreneur Christopher Lin, Jia has hired a consistently accomplished roster of designers, from East and West, to create a covetable range of kitchen- and tableware (Jia is the Mandarin word for 'home'). Even in this distinguished company, Jia's collaboration with Kate Chung and Italian designer Paola Navone to produce the limited-edition porcelain Emptiness Plates (above), HK$1,500 for a set of three, is a standout. Navone's hand-drawn black-and-white patterns are stark and intricate, and, proving functional tableware can be anything but domestic, are guaranteed to be the most arresting element of any kitchen shelf. You can purchase Jia Inc's wares at Haus Collection (T 2750 5571) at PMQ (see p037). *www.jia-inc.com*

Liger
HK style icons Dorothy Hui and Hilary
Tsui liken their store to a stroll through
their closets. The womenswear labels
on offer share a sense of edgy luxury,
from Korea's Pushbutton to the owners'
in-house brand, Oh My God. The neutral,
studio-like interior space ensures that
the clothing has plenty of room to shine.
Shop A & C, Vienna Mansion,
55 Paterson Street, T 2503 5308

Visual Culture

Less an optical shop than a temple to the humble pair of glasses, Visual Culture has brought to Asia the best in hand-crafted, heritage-rich global eyewear labels, such as Preciosa, Shuron and MOSCOT Originals. Its flagship store in Causeway Bay is stylish and spacious, lined with display cases set neatly against exposed concrete walls and framed by soft lighting. It also contains a few thoughtful surprises, including an intimate outdoor garden where shoppers can catch their breath among a bevy of blooming flowers. Although the rarity of the brands on offer means that many frames don't come cheap, prices here are less inflated than elsewhere in the city, and the bargain lenses for which Hong Kong is known will help offset the expense. *21 Lan Fong Road, T 2881 8291, www.visualculture.com.hk*

Shine

This Causeway Bay outpost of Hong Kong's leading emporium of chic frequently stops window-shoppers dead in their tracks due to its futuristic interior, a collaboration between two local practices, NC Design & Architecture and The Laboratory for Explorative Architecture & Design (LEAD). The delicate white exterior gives way to a monochrome display space, punctuated by an undulating ceiling that is covered with more than 900 pieces of interwoven cord, creating a spectacular moire pattern. None of this would matter, of course, if the selection on offer was found wanting, but Shine has firmly established itself as the go-to store for pioneering women's and menswear labels, such as sought-after shoe brand Camilla Skovgaard.

Shop B, Ground floor, 5-7 Cleveland Street, T 2890 8261, www.shinegroup.com.hk

The Armoury

Opened in 2010 by a multinational trio with a passion for classical styling, The Armoury bills itself as a seller of 'artisanal clothing'. It's a one-stop shop for the city's discerning and vaguely nostalgic urban gentlemen. An interior of lustrous wood and Victorian-looking furniture gives it the ambience of a private club that happens to stock some of the best suits, shoes, bags and accessories in town. Its extensive off-the-shelf selection leans heavily on handmade craftsmanship, spanning hats from London's Lock & Co to carved shoehorns from Abbeyhorn and polo shirts from Hong Kong maker Ascot Chang. If you can't find what you're after, the store's considerable international connections enable it to offer a range of bespoke and made-to-measure services. *307 Pedder Building, 12 Pedder Street, T 2804 6991, www.thearmoury.com*

Tang Tang Tang Tang

Fashion and retail impresario David Tang, owner of the retro-meets-dayglo Shanghai Tang label, isn't known for subtlety. But his new lifestyle and homewares venture is showy even by his standards. Set in a former pawn shop, its liberal splashes of imperial yellow, its marble floors and its hanging scrolls are a statement of opulent intent. The layout of the store mimics a Hong Kong home, complete with China-themed products that run the gamut from kitchenwares to furniture. The collection is preoccupied with design and indulgence, whether it's fortune cookie-shaped salt-and-pepper shakers or plush 'sleep shirts' embroidered with the Chinese zodiac. This should appeal to China's new aspirational class, which is the brand's primary target.
66 Johnston Road, T 2525 2112,
www.tangtangtangtang.com

Wai Yuen Tong

Do you feel rundown? Worried about the viscosity of your blood? Try some giant caterpillar fungus blended with dried deer-tail tea. This exotic remedy and countless others can be found at the immaculately presented Wai Yuen Tong Chinese medicine outlets – established in Guangzhou in 1897, relocated to HK in the post-revolutionary turmoil of the 1950s and given a complete makeover by local firm Another Design in 2008. All the packaging was revived in Sino red, oranges, yellows and pastel greens and blues; and chief designer Pal Pang introduced a sense of micromanaged order to the shop floor, where wooden drawer systems are installed behind every counter and the medicinal remedies are meticulously arranged in jars and cases.
Room 2, 88-89 Des Voeux Road,
T 2581 1980, www.waiyuentong.com

Lane Crawford
The cutting-edge department store has had a city presence since 1850, and, in 2014, this 7,600 sq m flagship by Yabu Pushelberg became its fifth Hong Kong branch. Lane Crawford's IFC Mall outlet fuses fashion, art and lifestyle, its wares displayed in distinct 'environments', from acrylic-screened womenswear galleries (pictured) to a CD bar fitted with iPods. *IFC Mall, 8 Finance Street, T 2118 3388*

Kelly & Walsh

Looking at Kelly & Walsh's sleek outlet in the Pacific Place shopping complex, you would never guess its roots stretch back to colonial-era Shanghai, where it was first founded as a publisher of English-language books on the Far East. Warm lighting, worn leather chairs and some unadorned wooden shelves encourage readers to explore a carefully curated selection of work that seems to celebrate all the key elements of good living – fine cuisine, exotic travel, fast automobiles. There's a particular emphasis on fashion, architecture and design, and even if you're not buying, browsing these huge coffee-table tomes full of visual candy from the likes of fashion designer Rick Owens and various Asia-based producers is a delight.

204, Level 2, Pacific Place, 88 Queensway, T 2522 5743, www.swindonbooks.com

General Store

Unabashedly retro, General Store is set in the middle of a wet market and occupies one of the spit-and-sawdust shophouses that are so prevalent in Hong Kong, yet rarely contain trendsetting retail. Step inside here, however, and you could be forgiven for thinking you've stumbled on someone's attic, or a museum. The shop is piled from floor-to-ceiling with vintage wooden furniture, ageing prints, old appliances, industrial lighting and knick-knacks – sourced from antiques shops around the world by owner Shelly Hayashi and her partner. Amid the rubble there are some newer pieces, including Noguchi 'Akari' lamps and wallpaper by Deborah Bowness. There's a real sense of discovery that makes visiting here a delight.
Shop H, 41 Gauge Street, T 2851 8144, www.generalstoreltd.com

SPORTS AND SPAS
WORK OUT, CHILL OUT OR JUST WATCH

The options for exercising outdoors in Hong Kong depend on what season it is. From November to March is perfect – the days are almost spring-like and running is a pleasure. The Peak Circle Walk and the path alongside the harbour in Kowloon get packed with joggers, early and late, and the 14 tennis courts in Victoria Park (1 Hing Fat Street, T 2570 6186) are also very popular. There is no better time to be in the city. Throughout the rest of the year, it can be a little bit more hit and miss, particularly when the humidity becomes unbearable. The typhoon season falls between April and October, when even the horse racing takes a break (in August), and you might want to consider transferring all activities indoors.

Fortunately, there is plenty of choice. Hotel spas in Hong Kong are as good as any in the world, and the offerings at The Peninsula (see p020), Landmark Mandarin Oriental (see p028) and the Four Seasons (see p030) are top class. Tempting alternatives include a hydrating facial treatment with cucumber and green tea, and a soothing hand massage for stressed-out smartphone thumbs at the Grand Hyatt's 7,500 sq m Plateau Spa (11th floor, 1 Harbour Road, T 2584 7688), or the Hotel Icon's Angsana Spa (see p093). Watersports are also beneficial. The best operators, such as Kayak-and-Hike (T 9300 5197, www.kayak-and-hike.com), offer trips to beaches and coves that you wouldn't normally stumble upon.
For full addresses, see Resources.

Shek O Beach

After indulging in dim sum and taking in your thousandth variation of the city view, you may feel that it's time to step away from the urban environment for a little sun and sea action. Shek O is one of the best beaches in Hong Kong and just getting there is a fun drive out to the east. If you're feeling energetic, you can hike up Dragon's Back to enjoy the vista over the Shek O strand and some of the Island's priciest real estate. Eating options are a bit basic, although Shek O Chinese & Thai Seafood Restaurant (T 2809 4426) has its fans and will do the job if you skipped lunch. There are also a handful of bars and cafés in Shek O town where you can grab a cold beer and take in the quaint, village-like vibe. Shining Stone (T 2809 2227) and Ben's Bar (T 2809 2268), on a secluded back beach, are two mellow mainstays.

Happy Valley Racecourse
This is the one unmissable slice of sport you have to catch in the city. The sense that you're right at the heart of the action, and that serious fortunes are being waged, is palpable. Take your seat in the open-air grandstand or at the Stable Bend Terrace for the early evening races on Wednesdays, and Saturday and Sunday in the daytime, surrounded by an urban jungle of towers.
2 Sports Road, T 3690 3690

Torq Cycle

The first fitness studio in Hong Kong dedicated exclusively to spinning, Torq opened in 2013 and manages to squeeze a lot into a limited city-centre space. Rows of stationary bicycles are lined up to face a massive computerised display that tracks cyclists' speed and progress, which, along with high-energy mixes from an in-house DJ, provides motivation and a competitive edge to workouts. Classes, or 'rides', can be purchased either as singles (HK$250) or in bundles, and exercise sessions blend cycling with Pilates, yoga and *Muay Thai* to ensure that the entire body is exhausted. Thankfully, the locker rooms, which have stone surfaces, rainfall showers, scented candles and chic toiletries from Australian brand Aesop, are a fitting reward.

26th floor, LiDong Building, 9 Li Yuen Street East, T 2677 8623, www.torqcycle.com

Angsana Spa

The Angsana, opened in 2011 and located within the boutique Hotel Icon (see p025), attempts to inject a bit of tropical warmth into Hong Kong's often austere spa scene. There are four generously sized therapy rooms (Camelia Treatment Room, above), each with individual showers and resting areas, brightened by displays of radiant flowers and sunny lime-green, tangerine, and yellow accents. It's luxury of a level you'd expect from the sister brand of the esteemed Banyan Tree. Treatments – such as the two-hour couples' Duet (HK$1,800 per person), which includes a body polish as well as a massage – draw heavily on the Angsana's roots in South-East Asia, and incorporate natural ingredients such as jasmine, sesame oil and bamboo.
Ninth floor, Hotel Icon, 17 Science Museum Road, T 3400 1052, www.hotel-icon.com

Flawless
Hong Kong has no shortage of spas but,
as most strive to evoke Bangkok or Bali,
few it could call its own. Enter Flawless,
which takes inspiration from the city's
design savvy and abundance of grit.
Treatments are conventional, focusing
on facials, manicures, pedicures and
massages, all impeccably executed.
*Fourth floor, Sea Bird House,
22-28 Wyndham Street, T 2869 5868*

ESCAPES

WHERE TO GO IF YOU WANT TO LEAVE TOWN

There's so much to do in Hong Kong and, surprisingly for such an urban centre, so many great beaches and green spaces to explore. When one does need to escape, however, the vast hinterland of China-proper beckons. Connections to the mainland will improve with a high-speed train line, due in 2015 but facing delays, which should cut travel times to Beijing to about 10 hours. Just over the border, Shenzhen is now the kind of low-cost retail destination Hong Kong used to be, yet, due to the arrival of bold architecture such as the Vanke Center (see p102), OMA's Stock Exchange (5045 Shennan East Road) and hotels like the Four Seasons (138 Fu Hua Third Road, Futian, T +86 755 8826 8888), it's fostering an air of sophistication. Another must-visit is Macau (see p100), a former Portuguese colony some 45 minutes away on the 1970s-fabulous hydrofoil. Gambling is de rigueur here, but it's also worth viewing the 18th-century neoclassical Leal Senado (Avenida de Almeida Ribeiro). Browse the shops along Rua de São Paulo; the Old House Gallery (No 27-27a, T +853 2835 8387) stocks mainland antiques.

Then there's Taipei, the Taiwanese capital with big ambitions. Take the 100-minute flight and stay at the glamorous Hotel Quote (333 Nanjing East Road, T +886 221 755 588). A similar distance away, the island of Hainan (opposite) is a beach getaway with an increasingly plush coterie of hotels and resorts.
For full addresses, see Resources.

The Ritz-Carlton, Sanya

An hour-and-a-half from Hong Kong by air, the semi-tropical island of Hainan is the focus of a major development push by the Chinese authorities, who hope to transform it into an Asian Hawaii. Unfortunately, this has resulted in overcrowded beaches and plenty of faceless chain hotels. The Ritz-Carlton's sumptuous Sanya retreat is an exception. Set in a secluded part of Yalong Bay, its Summer Palace-inspired buildings overlook spotless sands and are backed by thickly forested hills. Book one of the private Ocean Front Villas, which have their own gardens, plunge pools and outdoor pavilions. Amenities include seven dining options – Scene (above) offers Asian bites and classic cocktails. *Yalong Bay National Resort District, Hainan, T +86 898 8898 8888, www.ritzcarlton.com*

Yuzi Paradise, Guilin

A popular weekend getaway, known for its dramatic limestone hills, the Chinese city of Guilin was gifted with a less natural attraction in 2003, when a contemporary art park backed by a Taiwanese tycoon opened rather incongruously in its rural hinterland. Yuzi Paradise – or literally, 'fool's paradise', a cheeky poke at all those people who questioned the sanity of the undertaking – has blanketed an expansive patch of land with hundreds of sculptural installations that are set around buildings, pathways and natural lakes, combining works from China and abstract flights of fancy from Western luminaries such as Gheorghi Filin. Club Med manages a pair of luxurious properties on site, making it easy to stay here and take everything in.

Dabu Town, Yanshan, Guangxi,
T + 86 773 225 5000, www.yuzile.com

Macau

First, Stanley Ho's stranglehold on the casino trade was broken. Then came the rise of the Chinese middle class. Now, Macau, the Vegas of the East, is raising the stakes even higher. This small island currently rakes in more money than its US counterpart, and the land reclamation and resort development continues at a furious pace. Entertainment complex Fisherman's Wharf (T +853 8299 3300) contains a simulacrum of human history, from ancient Rome to Renaissance Venice, art deco Miami and French Quarter New Orleans. If the gambling isn't thrilling enough, you can bungee jump from the 338m Macau Tower (pictured; T +853 2893 3339). Visit at the weekend to witness the mainland *tai-pans* arrive with their suitcases packed full of cash. *www.macautourism.gov.mo*

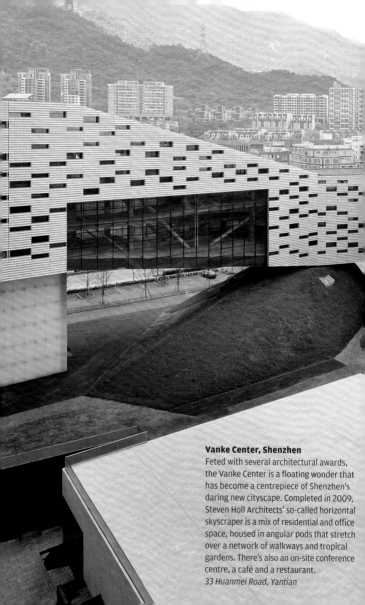

Vanke Center, Shenzhen

Feted with several architectural awards, the Vanke Center is a floating wonder that has become a centrepiece of Shenzhen's daring new cityscape. Completed in 2009, Steven Holl Architects' so-called horizontal skyscraper is a mix of residential and office space, housed in angular pods that stretch over a network of walkways and tropical gardens. There's also an on-site conference centre, a café and a restaurant.

33 Huanmei Road, Yantian

NOTES

SKETCHES AND MEMOS

RESOURCES
CITY GUIDE DIRECTORY

HOTELS
ADDRESSES AND ROOM RATES

Four Seasons 030
Room rates:
double, from HK$5,170;
Deluxe Harbour-View Room, HK$5,720
8 Finance Street
T 3196 8888
www.fourseasons.com/hongkong

Four Seasons Shenzhen 096
Room rates:
double, from ¥1,960
138 Fu Hua Third Road
Futian
Shenzhen
T +86 755 8826 8888
www.fourseasons.com/shenzhen

Hullett House 016
Room rates:
double, from HK$16,500
1881 Heritage
2a Canton Road
T 3988 0000
www.hulletthouse.com

Hotel Icon 025
Room rates:
double, from HK$4,840;
Club 36 Harbour, HK$8,030
17 Science Museum Road
T 3400 1000
www.hotel-icon.com

Hotel Indigo 016
Room rates:
double, from HK$1,900
246 Queen's Road East
T 3926 3888
www.hotelindigo.com

J Plus 016
Room rates:
double, from HK$3,520
1-5 Irving Street
T 3196 9000
www.jplushongkong.com

The Jervois 017
Room rates:
double, from HK$2,200;
Two-Bedroom Suite, HK$4,200
89 Jervois Street
T 3994 9000
www.thejervois.com

Landmark Mandarin Oriental 028
Room rates:
double, from HK$5,600;
L450 Deluxe, HK$5,800
15 Queen's Road
T 2132 0188
www.mandarinoriental.com/landmark

Mira Moon 018
Room rates:
double, from HK$4,000;
New Moon King Room, from HK$6,000
388 Jaffe Road
T 2643 8888
www.miramoonhotel.com

The Peninsula 020
Room rates:
double, from HK$4,080;
Grand Deluxe Kowloon View Room,
from HK$5,480
Salisbury Road
T 2920 2888
www.peninsula.com

Pentahotel 016
  Room Rates:
  double, from HK$1,170
  19 Luk Hop Street
  T 3112 8222
  www.pentahotels.com
The Putman 022
  Room rates:
  studio suite, from HK$1,210;
  One-Bedroom Suite, HK$2,860
  202 Queen's Road Central
  T 2233 2233
  www.theputman.com
Hotel Quote 096
  Room rates:
  double, from TWD10,450
  333 Nanjing East Road
  Taipei
  Taiwan
  T + 886 221 755 588
  www.hotel-quote.com
The Ritz-Carlton 016
  Room rates:
  double, from HK$4,700
  ICC
  1 Austin Road West
  T 2263 2263
  www.ritzcarlton.com
The Ritz-Carlton Sanya 097
  Room rates:
  double, from ¥4,000;
  Ocean Front Villa, from ¥21,800
  Yalong Bay National Resort District
  Sanya
  Hainan
  T +86 898 8898 8888
  www.ritzcarlton.com

The Upper House 024
  Room rates:
  double, from HK$4,500;
  Upper Suite, HK$15,000;
  Penthouse, HK$30,000
  Pacific Place
  88 Queensway
  T 2918 1838
  www.upperhouse.com
W 016
  Room rates:
  double, from HK$3,300
  1 Austin Road West
  T 3717 2222
  www.starwoodhotels.com
YMCA 016
  Room rates:
  double, from HK$1,355
  41 Salisbury Road
  T 2268 7000
  www.ymcahk.org.hk

WALLPAPER* CITY GUIDES

Executive Editor
Rachael Moloney

Editor
Ella Marshall

Authors
Jonathan Hopfner
Sharon Leece

Art Editor
Eriko Shimazaki
Original Design
Loran Stosskopf
Map Illustrator
Russell Bell

Photography Editor
Elisa Merlo
Assistant Photography Editor
Nabil Butt

Production Manager
Vanessa Todd-Holmes

Chief Sub-Editor
Nick Mee
Sub-Editor
Farah Shafiq

Editorial Assistants
Emilee Jane Tombs
Blossom Green

Interns
Sara Gonzato
Rosemary Stopher

Wallpaper* ® is a
registered trademark
of IPC Media Limited

First published 2007
Revised and updated
2010, 2011, 2013 and 2014

© Phaidon Press Limited

All prices are correct at
the time of going to press,
but are subject to change.

Printed in China

Phaidon Press Limited
Regent's Wharf
All Saints Street
London N1 9PA

Phaidon Press Inc
65 Bleecker Street
New York, NY 10012

Phaidon® is a registered
trademark of Phaidon
Press Limited

www.phaidon.com

A CIP Catalogue record for
this book is available from
the British Library.

ISBN 978 0 7148 6828 8

PHOTOGRAPHERS

Iwan Baan
Vanke Center, pp102-103

Jonathan de Villiers
HighCliff, pp010-011
Central Park Towers, p012
Happy Valley
Racecourse, pp090-091
Macau, pp100-101

Marcel Lam
Hong Kong city view,
inside front cover
ICC, p013
Two IFC, p014
One Peking, p015
Mira Moon, pp018-019
The Peninsula, p020, p021
Hotel Icon, p025,
pp026-027
Four Seasons, pp030-031
Konzepp, p033
Liang Yi Museum,
pp034-035
22 Ships, p036
PMQ, p037
Ammo, pp038-039
Duddell's, p041
The Pawn, pp042-043
Nocturne, p044

Yardbird, p045
Quinary, p048, p049
Ozone, pp050-051
Serge et le Phoque, p052
Lung King Heen, p053
Boqueria, pp056-057
Ronin, p058
Dragon-i, pp060-061
Anais-Jourden Mak Chun
Ting, p063
Landmark East, p065
Jockey Club Innovation
Tower, pp066-067
Jardine House, p068
Bank of China Tower, p069
Hong Kong Design
Institute, pp070-071
Liger, pp074-075
Visual Culture, p076, p077
Shine, pp078-079
The Armoury, p080
Tang Tang Tang Tang, p081
Wai Yuen Tong, pp082-083
Lane Crawford, pp084-085
Kelly & Walsh, p086
General Store, p087
Shek O Beach, p089
Torq Cycle, p092
Angsana Spa, p093
Flawless, pp094-095

Jillian Mitchell
Yuzi Paradise, pp098-099

Joyce Wang
Mott 32, p059

Michael Weber
The Jervois, p017

HONG KONG

A COLOUR-CODED GUIDE TO THE HOT 'HOODS

WEST KOWLOON
HK's grand-scale building development has been inspired by the world's best view

TSIM SHA TSUI
Check out 1881 Heritage – a high-end hotel, dining and shopping hub on the waterfront

CAUSEWAY BAY/HAPPY VALLEY
Visit the smart stores of Causeway Bay before having a flutter at the Happy Valley races

MID-LEVELS
Ride the Victoria Peak escalator with the execs and jump off to browse Soho's shops

CENTRAL
Find upmarket retail and nightlife among the financial district's riot of high-rises

ABERDEEN/STANLEY PENINSULA
Head to the south of the Island for a break from the city and a relaxed day on the beach

For a full description of each neighbourhood, see the Introduction.
Featured venues are colour-coded, according to the district in which they are located.